Saving Money

Simple tips that will help you save more money every day, and have more money every week!

Table of Contents

Introduction iv

Chapter 1: What Makes Saving Seem Impossible .. 1

Chapter 2: The Simplest Ways to Save Money 3

Chapter 3: Avoiding Splurges When Low on Cash 7

Chapter 4: Saving Money at Home and Work 10

Chapter 5: Saving Money Without Cutting Expenses 13

Chapter 6: Credits Cards, Debts and Finances 16

Chapter 7: How to Spend Excess Savings Wisely 20

Conclusion 23

Introduction

I want to thank you and congratulate you for downloading the book, *"Saving Money"*.

This book contains helpful information about saving money, and how you can easily begin having more in your account at the end of each week.

The majority of people in today's society struggle to save. We all seem to want the newest and the best, even if we can't afford it. Credit cards and loans are leading people to financial ruin, and even worse, schools aren't teaching us how to save properly either.

In this book we will cover simple steps that will help you begin saving, and change your attitudes to money in the process. Money is an abundant resource, and we need to realize there is plenty to go around. Once you have some savings, it's easy to turn it in to more and more money in a short time. Whether through a business, real-estate, stock market, or some other form of investing you can make a lot more money once you have some initial savings.

Here, you will learn the skills that will have you successfully saving, and if you follow the steps laid out in this book you will be one step closer to financial freedom.

This book will explain to you tips and techniques that will help you successfully reduce your expenses and save more of your hard earned cash. I hope this book is able to help you, please approach this subject with an open mind and I urge you to give these steps ago!

Thanks again for downloading this book, I hope you enjoy it!

Chapter 1: What Makes Saving Seem Impossible

It's normal to spend money on a daily basis, but what's not normal is not noticing that some of these expenses are actually more impulsive than necessary. In this book, you will learn about the simplest ways to save money, what are the usual culprits for not being able to save, and further tips on cutting costs efficiently.

Why Do We End Up Wasting Money?

Nobody really likes to waste money. If given a clean chance to, you would really like to save or set aside money for more important things. What people have trouble with is finding that "clean chance" to start saving. Oftentimes there are small windows opening, giving way to a chance to save up. However, 90% of the time people fail to take it. Why do people fail to take the small and frequent chances to save up?

1. Believing There's Always Another Time for Saving

It's common for people to put off saving because they are either already in the middle of a financial crisis or simply caught up in a shopping spree. It could also be said that people don't feel financially secure, so they think that starting to save might just make things difficult. What happens is the development of this mindset – "I can start later." Sometimes, this "later" never comes, or when it does, there are emergencies and other more pressing financial matters need attention. In the end, there's really no better time to start saving than now.

2. Letting Money Run its Own Course

Without organized finances and set goals, people end up buying things they want randomly and impulsively. Oftentimes, because people put off saving, they are unable to produce money to buy whatever they set out to purchase. It takes months, if not weeks, for them to produce the right amount to afford what they need. Sometimes, their goals are pushed so far from their expected deadline or, in some occasions, even entirely forgotten.

3. Thinking Independence/ Not Being Tied Down Doesn't Require Saving

People with families are not the only ones who should think about saving money. At some point in your life, you will grow old, become obsolete in your career or simply experience financial difficulties. During these trying times, you will wish you had some "backup" stored up somewhere to help you survive. Aside from that, just because you are flying solo, it doesn't mean that the things you buy impulsively doesn't add up to much. It might surprise you but most single (not in a relationship) individuals spend twice as much, if not equivalent, as a person who has children or a family. Weekly take-out dinners, designer clothes, exclusive DVD sets, and entertainment systems are infinitely more expensive than a month's worth of diapers.

Chapter 2: The Simplest Ways to Save Money

Saving money daily can actually come as easily as eating breakfast or deciding to walk instead of taking the bus to school. What's difficult is realizing these small ways of saving money. It's easy to overlook something so simple, and mistake it for something tacky or menial. In saving money, these simple and daily acts won't just keep your bill neatly in your wallet, they might also double it by the end of the week.

Here are some of the most overlooked but obvious habits you should learn in order to save money every day:

Fold it, Put it in your Pocket, and Keep it there

One of the best and most commonly quoted advice about saving money is this: "The best way to double your money is by folding it in half and putting it in your pocket." In reality, literally, folding your money bill in half won't double its amount. However, the total value of what you have *can* and *will* be doubled for each day you follow this habit successfully. If, for example, in each day you set aside five dollars without touching or scheming to spend it on something, by the end of the week you would have added 35 dollars to your savings.

HOW IT HELPS:

Folding your money over or simply keeping it in your pocket won't just save you some money, it will help control those shopping impulses. One of the most common mistakes people make when they get their money on payday is splurging. It's no surprise if you can relate to a scene like this – pay day arrives and you feel as rich as a king. It only takes a week, or less, of seemingly endless wealth until you're broke or nearly broke. By the end of the month, you're sulking, cutting down expenses and waiting at the edge of your seat for the next payday. The cycle happens and it will continue to happen over and over again until you decide to act upon it.

Saving Every Penny

Most people think of small bills as insignificant because, well, they are *small* or have less value and would not really be of any use in emergencies. The truth is, they are actually the most significant portion of the idea of "savings".

HOW IT HELPS:

Small amounts are what a person builds up and turns into millions. Mountains are not made of singular gigantic boulders. They are made of sand, stones, rocks and *some* boulders. In the financial comparison of mountains to savings, it's the pennies that make up the base and not the hundreds. While saving pennies wont make you rich, it will change your relationship with money. If you practice putting your coins in a tin every day, you will condition yourself to save. This brings us to the next overlooked technique in saving money, for long- or short-term purposes.

Starting Small and Starting Now

Starting small is the easiest way to save, but starting small is belittled by most because of the expected value it achieves. "Every little bit counts," that's one saying that applies to a lot of things, including saving money. Since the idea of saving up is a continuous and consistent habit, even the small contributions add up to the pile. It's also easy to save by starting small, because it gives people enough freedom to buy the things they need or want. It won't feel like such a responsibility, which will lengthen its chances of actually growing to be a successful habit.

HOW IT HELPS:

The benefit is simple, relating to saving each penny. The sooner you start saving, no matter how small the beginnings, the more chances you'd have to accumulate your wealth.

Develop Financial Strategies

Plan your expenses or, in a much better sense, strategize. When allowances or salaries come, you always have the urge to buy things you've fantasized about during times of financial "drought".

HOW IT HELPS:

If you already have cash allocated for both these urges and the debts that need to be cleared, you won't get off course and get lost in your financial system. In other words, you won't get a migraine from piled up bills or worry if your next salary won't just end up as a payment for debts.

Chapter 3: Avoiding Splurges When Low on Cash

During the times of financial drought or difficulties, one can't help but fantasize on objects, activities, food, and other things that can't be had. It's one of the human race's natural flaws – to want something that's impossible to have. When someone is broke or is cutting down on expenses heavily, there's this feeling of being limited.

What Lack of Money Can Do to People

While it's true that some people are limited financially, it's not true that they are limited in happiness. However, money can buy almost anything that can make someone happy, *instantly*. This is the problem – instant. People seek instant pleasure and spending your money is always the solution. So, whenever someone is short of money, that person feels deprived of this instant happiness that other people are getting. There is envy and there is an increasing desire to have something as soon as possible. It's like an addiction, so by the time the money arrives, people are so hungry to spend that they are able to do it daily without thinking about their budget.

How to Avoid Overspending and Spending Wrongly

There are some easy ways to avoid overspending, but the most effective ones are difficult to do and will need commitment.

LEARN TO CONTROL URGES

The simplest but most difficult and complicated solution is to control it. Not just when the money is finally available, but even when there is financial scarcity. It's natural to *want* things, but it's important to know if this desire is beneficial in the long run. True, that those boxes of cupcakes from the delicacy store last week are screaming for attention, and so are your taste buds, but are there no other options to satisfy your cravings without spending as much?

Sometimes people get blinded by *the idea* more than its purpose. Going back to the "cupcakes" example, a lot of items and foods on the market today are overpriced. Most of them have high prices because they are popular, branded, or are served in the comfort of a very fancy interior. The idea of sitting down in a restaurant that's adorned with shiny wooden walls and has a live band is sometimes more alluring than the idea of getting food to satiate hunger itself.

BUY WISELY BY BUYING FAIRLY-PRICED ITEMS

Try aiming for simple but fairly priced offerings. Let your cravings, desires, and decisions to save meet half way. Make a relationship out of them and learn to commit accordingly. In saving money, nobody is forced to save or banned from spending on pricey items. All you have to do is *wisely choose what and where to spend money on.* Most things are short-lived or forgotten easily, if you're going to spend a great deal of valuable money on something, that something should be just as valuable – both financially and personally.

LET YOURSELF SPEND FREELY SOMETIMES

Give yourself your own allowance for splurging and going wild in the mall. What makes most people end up spending more than they intend to, is that they are deprived or restricted from buying even the simplest things they desire. Being held back for so long, people unknowingly unleash the monstrous spendthrift within when the budget comes in. To prevent this feeling of restriction, give yourself some freedom to spend, but do take note of the word "some". You have to learn to appreciate this freedom and control urges that could very well make you broke for the rest of the month.

ALLOCATE ACCORDINGLY

Don't restrict yourself when saving by leaving out only a little of what you earn. Instead, plan ahead and "cut" your money in portions. It can be 15% for the savings, 40% for house expenses, another 30% for transportation costs and daily expenses, and the remaining 15% for anything you wish to buy.

CUT DOWN ON CERTAIN EXPENSES

Cut down on other areas as compensation, especially those that you feel have grown excessive. This way, you'll have a much larger financial freedom and at the same time not be pressured by other responsibilities.

AVOID CATCHING THE SALE/DISCOUNT HYPE

Discounts and sales are great, but not when you're cutting costs. If it's possible, save up for these store sales by not spending on miscellaneous items. If that cocktail dress or game console is really catching your eye more times than you allow yourself, it means it's about time to plan on saving up for it. In order for that to happen, focus the money solely unto that. So, when the time comes that a discount or sale is up, you'll be able to buy it for less and maybe even have some left for an accessory.

Chapter 4: Saving Money at Home and Work

Aside from the usual techniques in saving money, like keeping it in your pocket, there are plenty other ways to cut down costs effectively. It's not just miscellaneous expenses or keeping yourself from getting broke that's getting in the way of effective saving. Some things at home, like electricity and food, contribute to your financial responsibilities.

Money Saving Tips at Home and at Work

Saving money at home and at work is more than possible, and doing so is very helpful and practical. Those unused lights in the room or the unnecessary air conditioning – they will help lower the electric bill once turned off.

SAVING ON FOOD:

- Bring your own water bottle to work or school. Drinking water is expensive, especially when you need to drink every now and then. If the office has a fridge in the pantry but has no drinking fountains, bringing your own water bottle can really cut costs.

- Packing your lunch is one obvious way of saving money. Fast food and dining at restaurants can chop off a great deal of your allowance if done on a regular basis. Imagine how much you could save by bringing your own lunch to work, even for just four days a week. Instead of just bringing your own water, why not go all the way and pack your own meal to save money.

- Refrigerate your leftovers. Wasted food is wasted money, so don't leave leftovers on the table because you will end up throwing it out. The more often you throw out food the more often you buy food, which obviously means spending more than necessary.

SAVING ON GAS/COMMUTE EXPENSES:

- If you have a bike at home, use it sometimes for doing errands that are close by. It will help save up on gas and also work you up a sweat. Some exercises will contribute to a healthier body, which in turn means fewer sick leaves and lower medical expenses.

- On days when there is not enough money to spend, consider staying in for dinner or using what money you have left to buy groceries. Instead of eating out, cook at home. Doing so will help you save on other related expenses, like getting gas for the car.

OTHER WAYS TO SAVE:

- Overspending on hygiene products is a big "no" for people who are hygiene conscious. Firstly, half of these products are usually forgotten when a more interesting one is found. Most beauty products at home are either still half full when new ones are bought. What happens is when they are discovered later on to be still useful, they are already expired and useless. Making hair shine and skin silk smooth might be a critical thing for most women, but it is advised to avoid buying more until the current products have been used up. If a certain beauty product does not seem to work well, don't just leave it at home – give it away to someone who might want it.

- A fun way of saving is putting a jar on the table near the door. When commuting or coming home, whatever change you have in your pocket, drop them into the jar. Make this a daily habit and, sooner or later, it will start to build up into a little treasure. It's also a great way of finding extra change in case you run out of money to pay the cab.

- Going over your monthly bills won't lessen them in an instant, but seeing how much you have spent so far will certainly make an impact. It might also give you an idea where to cut back on. It will also reveal more unpaid taxes and debts.

Chapter 5: Saving Money Without Cutting Expenses

There are some things that you can do to save without having to cut down your expenses or making your freedom money scarce. Here are some of the more daring money saving ideas you might want to incorporate in your saving plans:

EARNING EXTRA:

- Having a yard or backyard sale will teach people the value of things and money. There are some people who buy so many things and end up with a messy house of unused junk. Make a habit of cleaning out unused items before adding up new items that could end up in the stock room or backyard over time. Selling unused items or giving them away, even throwing out old objects, won't just make room for new items in the house. It will also allow you to earn some real cash to pay for home-improvement services.

- If earning more seems to be the most ideal way to boost your savings, consider working overtime at the office. If you have talents or other passions, then use these to acquire a sideline or a freelance job. These simple sideline jobs can become really helpful during times of need, they can also be your source of *freedom money.*

HOW TO SAVE ON GROCERIES AND OTHER EXPENSES:

- Try to buy generic medicine sometimes. What most people don't know or fail to believe is that generic medicines are just as potent as brand-name medicines. The difference mainly is that brand-name medicines are more expensive because of how much the company spends on advertisements, commercials, and other sales-boosting activities. Generic-drug companies don't spend on any of those. Both kinds of medicine are FDA-approved, which means you don't have to worry about generic brands being fake.

- Buying video games is a habit that no one can easily escape from, and it's an expensive habit too. The best way to compensate for this is to buy video games that actually have a great replay value. Choose games that have high ratings and that are still great to replay (especially those with extra content or hidden levels). Another great way to avoid overspending on video games is to avoid buying new ones until you have mastered what game you already have. Now that's a challenge a gamer should be able to take up enthusiastically.

- Consider alternating gym hours with jogging in the neighborhood. Keeping fit is part of most people's lifestyles, but gym fees or court entrance fees can be expensive for those who have a regular schedule. Jogging or brisk walking might not be as pleasantly punishing as a workout in the gym, but they do their part in keeping the body in tune.

HOW TO GET GOOD DEALS:

- Collect those coupons that might come in handy. You don't have to use the coupons immediately or go out of your way just so you can prove there's saved money in that. Save only the coupons that might be useful, especially those for groceries. When the time comes to buy eggs, a discount coupon might score you some great deals, providing a week's worth of breakfast.

- Buying online is not for everybody, but depending on the item and where it is available, online shopping could cut costs. Buying baby gear and furniture online, for example, is more efficient than going out to the mall. For one thing, it prevents you from adding extra stuff to the cart, things that aren't even on the list. It will also keep you from having to buy food, as shopping can make you hungry. It will also save you from having to gas up the car or pay for the commute. Lastly, there are often sales and great deals at online stores, much like in malls. As long as you are certain of the online store's credibility and quality of its products, then purchasing online will definitely be an easier and cheaper task than going out.

Chapter 6: Credits Cards, Debts and Finances

Money talk almost always involves debts and strategies on how to manage finances. Below are some helpful insights regarding each "money problem" and how to conquer its effects:

Take Advantage of Your Local Grocery's Membership Card

Make use of that membership card at the grocery store. People don't take up the opportunity to apply for membership cards at their local store, or simply put it off each time because of the fee. The truth is, the longer you put it off, the more you are missing out on unaccounted savings. If there's only one grocery store that you visit every time, then it's one obvious advantage for you to sign up. As for having a lot of memberships, learn to prioritize or let go.

Cancelling Unneeded Membership Cards

On another note, cancel memberships you rarely use or don't use at all. Some memberships are used, but not as much as they are supposed to. If you have the kind of membership that requires monthly payments but you are not able to benefit from it monthly, cancelling it will help. If a membership is paid on a yearly basis, try to at least make the most of the year and determine whether renewing the membership will be ideal. Regardless of the payment systems or benefits of becoming a member of some clubs or gyms, see whether you can really commit. Unused privileges are almost the same as unrefrigerated leftovers, as they are goods that are taken for granted.

Adjust Your Phone Line or Phone's Plan

Change your phone plan. It's not *always* useful to have access to the internet. If your home and office already have Wi-Fi internet connections, then getting 3G services for your phone will just be wasteful. Change your phone plan according to your needs. If it's part of your work to keep in touch with clients even at home, then a plan for unlimited calls can be helpful. Skip the additional add-ins that your phone company is offering, chances are they won't be used as much as they are meant to be.

Downgrading Your Cable

Change your cable plan. Chances are that only 20% of the 200 channels you had installed are watchable or appealing to you. If more than half of these channels are deemed useless or unseen, better downgrade to a more ideal plan. As long as your cable plan contains the channels that you need, like the news, sports, and some leisurely ones, you'll survive each day without the premiums.

Minimize the Use of Your Credit Card

Don't use your credit card for anything else besides an emergency. A romantic date is not an emergency, just to keep things clear. Medically related incidents are what usually fall under the category of emergency. Losing money on the way home, or getting robbed are emergencies. Only use credit cards when you absolutely need to, and only you can tell when exactly that is. People often overuse their credit cards and miscalculate how much they owe the company, ending up buried in debt. This also leads to another money saving reminder.

Clear Your Debts First

Pay off your debt. Credit card holders beware – pay your credit debts on time or else the interest will build up causing instant problems as opposed to the instant pleasures of credit card usage. Should the credit debts be unpaid for the month, avoid using it until the debt has been paid along with the interest. As much as possible, use your credit card sparingly, that is if you can't ultimately keep it away only for emergency purposes.

As for other necessary debts, like student loans, house loans, and business loans, as much as possible take care of them when you are able to. If you have a steady job, find a way to set aside some money in order to pay off the loan even in tiny amounts. Letting your loan build up in interest will just make them harder to pay off in the future. If it's possible, consult the bank or college where the loan has been granted, and seek alternative payment options. Some banks allow lower payment rates for longer periods of time, despite having the same interest as its more expensive and short-term payment counterparts.

Automated Savings Account

Automated savings could help you a lot. If you own a bank account and have an ATM card, you can apply for an automated savings account. It will automatically deduct a certain amount from your ATM card and transfer it into a savings account. Depending on the bank and its options, you are able to choose how much money will be automatically deducted from your ATM account and how frequently this will happen. A great way to schedule this automated savings is having it deduct from your account on the same day as your payday. This way, you can freely use the money you have in your ATM without having to worry about setting some aside for savings.

Set Goals and Plan Your Savings

Try to establish a timeframe for goals. For example, buying a new house or car is a goal that is more possible than ever. Saving up for it will be much easier if you set a deadline for it. If the goal is to get the house or car in three years' time, then you will be obliged to save as much as you can before that term reaches its end.

Plan out your savings, particularly in terms of how much to set aside each month, in order to meet your goals. Calculate how much to save each week, month, or year to reach the goal. While this isn't always followed strictly, at least it will allow you to compensate for each skipped deposit. The idea is to create a momentum and encourage consistency. It is one of the greatest secrets of saving.

Write Down Your Budget (And Stick to It)

Writing down your budget is almost the same as planning your savings. The difference is that you are setting financial boundaries for the necessities at home. While financial freedom is supposed to make you feel unrestricted, setting financial boundaries or a cash allocation will help you monitor how much electricity, food, and gas you use up. It will also implement a financial law where a certain amount of money is meant only for the electric bill and should not be used for anything else. The cash allocation will ensure that all your bills will be paid in time, if not in advance, minimizing or eliminating debts for good.

Chapter 7: How to Spend Excess Savings Wisely

There are some daring things you could try doing to boost the amount of your money. These are not necessary steps, but they are the most recommended actions to make use of extra savings, or to double them.

Invest in Stocks

Most people think that investment is only for rich people or those with high paying jobs. The truth is, investing can be for anyone, even minimum wage employees – as long as they have enough for a starter account. Investing in stocks is one good way of putting money where you can't touch it, there's also more growth in stocks than in a savings account, if cared for properly. Before plunging into this kind of investment step, ask, study, and learn the basics.

Invest in Your Skill

Investment doesn't just mean investing in a business or in the stocks. It can also pertain to an investment in your own talents. For example, you are a corporate worker who is secretly skilled in painting. If it's part of your dream to actually paint and sell your artwork, use a small portion of your savings to invest on some paints and brushes. It might seem like it's only for personal satisfaction, but personal satisfaction involving talent is always an investment. Once practiced and enhanced, your skill can be a means to earn more money through freelancing or part-time work.

Give to Charity

Give a little bit of money to charity. Of course, it technically falls on the spending category than on the saving category. This little action of charity, on the other hand, should better be understood as a tithe – an offering of thanks to the universe, if not a God, for the blessings. For some people, karma is real and what you give to the world returns to you tenfold. If this idea is not appealing, you can think of it as acting rich. Giving some to those in need doesn't always mean giving money to poor people or charities. These people in need could include your sister who is short on cash (but needs to buy something for her school project). These people in need can be your parents who, lingering for some time at the back of your head, you could please with some surprise gifts.

Acquire a Social Security

Apply for a social security system. It's going to provide your needs when you are old and can't work anymore. Some people won't have time for families or won't be able to have children, so when they do get old there might not be anyone to care for them. Although some families claim to love each other and are prepared to support each other, including financially, no matter what, there will still be instability and scarcity when a person has grown real old. A social security card might as well be your lifesaver once you feel that retirement is at hand.

Have Health or Life Insurance

Get insured, there's nothing wrong or paranoid about it. There is no telling what can happen in a person's life, and getting insured is a failsafe for most people with families and loved ones. Some insurance companies offer affordable contracts that provide refunds when their terms end and the deposits are unused. There is also a wide variety of life and medical insurances.

Treat Money as Sacred

Last and most especially, treat money as a sacred thing. It is something that comes and goes, but it never comes in the same way all the time. There are times of abundance and there are times of scarcity, you should be able to make the most of the plentiful times and save for the times when you will need it the most. It's true that money can be easy to come by, if you know how to earn it, but it's difficult to keep money.

Don't treat money as a means to get the things you want and need just for the moment. You should perceive money as a means of stability and security –built by saving and managing wisely, and not an instant solution to satisfying a temporary urge.

Conclusion

Thank you again for downloading this book!

I hope this book was able to help you learn more about saving money.

The next step is to put this information to use, and begin saving more money today! Remember to approach your finances strategically, and plan what expenses are necessary. Save daily to reinforce your new relationship with money. And lastly, saving doesn't have to be boring. Reward yourself along the way with planned expenses that still fit in to your overall savings scheme.

Good luck with your financial future, I hope this book was able to give you some new ideas for saving money, and changed your attitude to money in some way!

Finally, if you enjoyed this book, please take the time to share your thoughts and post a review on Amazon. It'd be greatly appreciated!

Thank you and good luck!